Superphonics **Storybooks** will help your child to learn to read using Ruth Miskin's highly effective phonic method. Each story is fun to read and has been carefully written to include particular sounds and spellings.

The Storybooks are graded so your child can progress with confidence from easy words to harder ones. There are four levels - Blue (the easiest), Green, Purple and Turquoise (the hardest). Each level is linked to one of the core *Superphonics Books*.

ISBN 0 340 80546 3

Text copyright © 2001 Clive Gifford
Illustrations copyright © 2001 Clive Scruton

Editorial by Gill Munton
Design by Sarah Borny

The rights of Clive Gifford and Clive Scruton to be identified as the author and illustrator of this Work have been asserted by them in accordance with the Copyright, Designs and Patents Act 1988.

First published in Great Britain 2001

10 9 8 7 6 5 4 3 2 1

First published i.
a division of Hodder Headline Limited,
338 Euston Road, London NW1 3BH

Printed by Wing King Tong, China

A CIP record is registered by and held at the British Library.

Target words

This Purple Storybook focuses on the following sounds:

oo as in **food** | **ew** as in **threw**
u-e as in **tune**

These target words are featured in the book:

beetroot	gloomy	school	Jude
boo	gooseberry	soon	prunes
boom	hoop	spoon	rude
boot	hooted	tooth	tube
boots	loomed	trooped	tune
broom	loop	Witchipoo	
broomstick	looped	Witchipoo's	brew
coo	moo	yoo-hoo	brewed
cooed	mood	zoomed	crew
cooing	mooed	zooming	flew
cool	mooing		new
doom	moon	blue	newts
food	moonbeams	clue	stew
fool	pools	duke's	threw
foolish	room	glue	
gloom	root	huge	

(Words containing sounds and spellings practised in the Blue and Green Storybooks and the other Purple Storybooks have been used in the story, too.)

Other words

Also included are some common words (e.g. **too**, **was**) which your child will be learning in his or her first few years at school.

A few other words have been included to help the story to flow.

Reading the book

1 Make sure you and your child are sitting in a quiet, comfortable place.

2 Tell him or her a little about the story, without giving too much away:

Jude doesn't like her school dinners - until she visits Witchipoo's school!

This will give your child a mental picture; having a context for a story makes it easier to read the words.

3 Read the target words (above) together. This will mean that you can both enjoy the story without having to spend too much time working out the words. Help your child to sound out each word (e.g. **b-r-oo-m**) before saying the whole word.

4 Let your child read the story aloud. Help him or her with any difficult words and discuss the story as you go along. Stop now and again to ask your child to predict what will happen next. This will help you to see whether he or she has understood what has happened so far.

Above all, enjoy the story, and praise your child's reading!

Ruth Miskin's

Superphonics

Purple Storybook

Witchipoo's School

by Clive Gifford

Illustrated by Clive Scruton

*Hodder
Children's
Books*

a division of Hodder Headline Limited

Jude was on her way home from school.

She was in a bad mood.

School dinner had been meat
which was as tough as old boots,
and cabbage with an awful smell
that filled the room.

Pudding had been prunes,
with custard as sticky as glue.

"I wish I could go to a new school,"
sighed Jude. "A school with good food!"

"I can fix that for you!"

Jude turned round.
An owl was sitting on the school gate.

"Owls can't talk!" said Jude.
She pulled a face at him.

"There's no need to be rude!"
hooted the owl. "I'm trying to help you.
If you want a new school -
just jump through this magic hoop!"

Jude frowned.
"A school with good food?" she asked.

"Oh, yes," hooted the owl, with a wink.

Jude felt a bit foolish –
but she did as the owl had said.

Soon she was zooming down
a long blue tube.

Cool!

She landed in a huge, gloomy room.

Water dripped from the walls,

and moonbeams gleamed

on the stone floor.

"Boo!" said a voice.

"My name is Witchipoo –

and this is my school!"

Witchipoo grinned at Jude.

"Is this really a school?" asked Jude.

Witchipoo loomed over her.

"Oh, yes!

It's a very special school.

Witchipoo always tells the truth!"

"Will we be eating soon?" asked Jude.

"Very soon!" cackled Witchipoo.

"But first you must meet my crew!"

Witchipoo clapped her hands
and shouted, "Yoo-hoo!"

A huge cat and a skinny black crow
loomed up out of the gloom.

"Say hello, you two!" cried Witchipoo.

"Coo! Coo!" cooed the cat.

"Moo! Moo!" mooed the crow.

"I'm testing a new spell on them,"
explained Witchipoo.

"Let's have a ride on my broomstick!"
cried Witchipoo.

The broomstick flew round the room.
It even looped the loop.

It was really cool!

"Now I'm going to make the stew,"
said Witchipoo.
"It has to be brewed before full moon.
It's called – the Stew of DOOM!"

Jude went white when she saw
what Witchipoo threw into the stew.

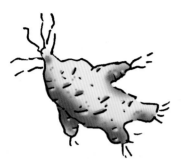

"A poison root and a duke's big toe,

Into my black pot they must go.

A smelly boot and the tooth of a snake,

Into the pot, my brew to make.

Two green newts and a rusty nail,

Add a few flies and a mouse's tail.

Stir three times with my magic spoon ...

And we have ALMOST brewed

the Stew of Doom!"

"ALMOST?" said Jude.

A chill ran up and down her spine.

Witchipoo's eyes were like black pools.

"Just one thing to add,
and that is YOU, little Jude!"

Jude didn't want to be part of a stew!

She made a dash for the door.

"Grab her!" screamed Witchipoo.

The cooing cat and the mooing crow chased Jude round the room.

The cat barred the way to the door.

The crow grabbed her hair with its beak.

Jude hadn't a clue how to get free.

"You didn't tell me the truth!
This isn't a school at all!" she cried.

"Foolish girl!
You fell into my trap!"
hissed Witchipoo.
"I needed a girl for my Stew of Doom!
You will go in the pot as soon as
we've sung the magic song!"

The cat started to coo a magic tune.

The mooing crow joined in.

Witchipoo jigged round the room,
singing:

"Boom! Boom!

A hat and a broom!

Soon I will eat the Stew of Doom!"

Jude gave the cat a hard push.

It crashed into Witchipoo,

and she fell into the pot of stew!

Jude grabbed the broomstick

and threw it at the crow.

Jude didn't hang around.

She zoomed out of the door.

"Jude! Over here!"

It was the owl!

Jude dived through the hoop –

just in time!

"So how did you like Witchipoo's School?" asked the owl, back at the school gate.

"Not very much," said Jude.

She couldn't wait to get back to her old school.

The next day, Jude and her class trooped in for dinner.

It was beetroot salad with boiled eggs as hard as rocks.

Pudding was lumpy gooseberry fool.

Jude ate every scrap.
It wasn't the best food in the world.
But it was better than the Stew of Doom!